The Hero Book

The Hero Book
an illustrated memoir

by Scott Waters

Cumulus PRESS

MONTRÉAL

Dépôt légal, Bibliothèque nationale du Québec, 4e trimèstre 2006.
Legal Deposit, National Library of Canada, 4th quarter 2006.

Library and Archives Canada Cataloguing in Publication

Waters, Scott, 1970-
    The hero book : an illustrated memoir / Scott Waters. -- 3rd ed.

ISBN 0-9733499-7-2

    I. Title.

PS8645.A844H47 2006   C813'.6   C2006-904270-5

designed & typeset by Chester Rhoder @ Typo-Pawsitive
everything else by Scott Waters

Printed in Gatineau, Québec by Imprimerie Gauvin. The b&w pages are printed on 100% post-consumer recycled paper, which was unavailable for the coated colour pages. We are trying to gain access to varying grades of 100% post-consumer recycled paper for future print runs.

Cumulus Press acknowledges the support of the Canada Council for the Arts for its publishing program.

 Canada Council   Conseil des Arts
for the Arts   du Canada

 Cumulus PRESS
P.O. Box 5205
Station B
Montréal (Québec) H3B 4B5
www.cumuluspress.com

For the members of 870 Tataryn.
Time heals all wounds—perhaps a little too well.

"One day one of their number would write a book about all this, but none of them would believe it, because none of them would remember it that way."
— James Jones

Also, for Shannon and her books.

Bern ordered a triple rye and coke and had just taken his first couple of sips when a *Squad NCO* arrived and, using the physical force of his snarling voice, propelled us out of the airport lounge and onto the bus.

Arriving at the Halifax Airport in group after group over a four-day period, we—no longer civvies but not yet soldiers—were shunted onto green Canadian Forces-branded coaches and driven the four or so hours to the famed Annapolis Valley and *CFB Cornwallis*.

Departing from Halifax, we arrived at Cornwallis in the dark, and just like the narrator in Samuel Butler's utopic novel, *Erewhon*, we were completely at a loss for level ground as the *NCO* screamed at us to get the fuck off the bus. Under the all too appropriately overcast night sky we were gathered together on the wet roadway in a sad approximation of a formation. There we stood motionless for half an hour until our own *Squad NCO* arrived and berated us into the communal barracks that would subsume our former selves.

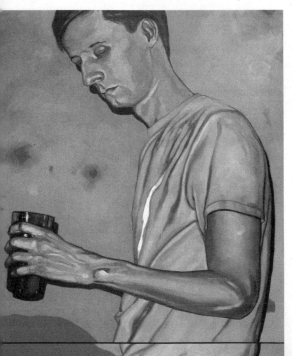

At an expected—but no less traumatic—early hour, we were woken by garbage cans pounding on the steel frames of our bunk beds. "Oh my God, what have I done?" was my first thought on this first morning of becoming an infantry soldier.

**Important
Notes on
The Nature of
Utopic Spaces**:

One of the first phases of military indoctrination is
disorientation with the end goal being reconstruction.
Contrary to some mythologies, you never lose your sense
of being an individual—automatons are not effective when
combat calls—but what you have previously accepted as
individuality is restructured so that the self now exists for
the benefit of the group. That is not such a bad thing and
sometimes feels like the ideal form of surrender.

More than truisms such as "breaking you down and building
you up," the military, first and foremost, needs to physically and
psychologically separate you from what is known*. It's a classic
trope of utopian texts; first the voyager must transit through
a nether realm, be it shipwreck, snowstorm, leisurely nap or, in
the case of Louis Marin's analysis of Disneyland, the monorail.
To move from one set of norms to another, the utopic quest
requires a neutral space to set loose the traveler's anchor.

* Due to logistical banalities this initial traversing of the neutral space
isn't always possible. Aaron, for example, lived just down the road
from the base. His folks dropped him off at the front gate with all the
spectacle of going to the mall for an afternoon. Really though, as soon as
you cross the gate, the world warps into a new version of itself, bus trip
or no.

Anthony Swofford writes about how his **USMC** recruiter would go for runs with him and come over for family dinners, all in the name of adding bodies to the ranks.

Back in the day, Canada could probably neither afford such extravagance nor safely offer a face which actively places killing alongside turkey and stuffing. We did, however, receive a complimentary lunch at any local restaurant after writing the Canadian Forces aptitude test.

Lying is free and easy though. I'm pretty good at it and the **CF** recruiters dedicate themselves to it.

"What's that son? Oh, sure, if you don't like it just get out. Or change from the infantry into another trade. It's really easy."

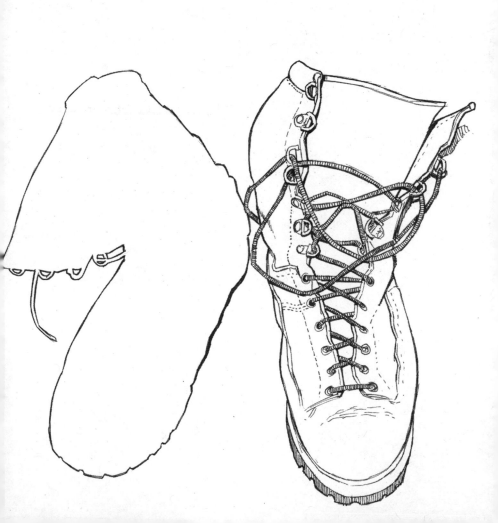

"All Jocks Stand Up."

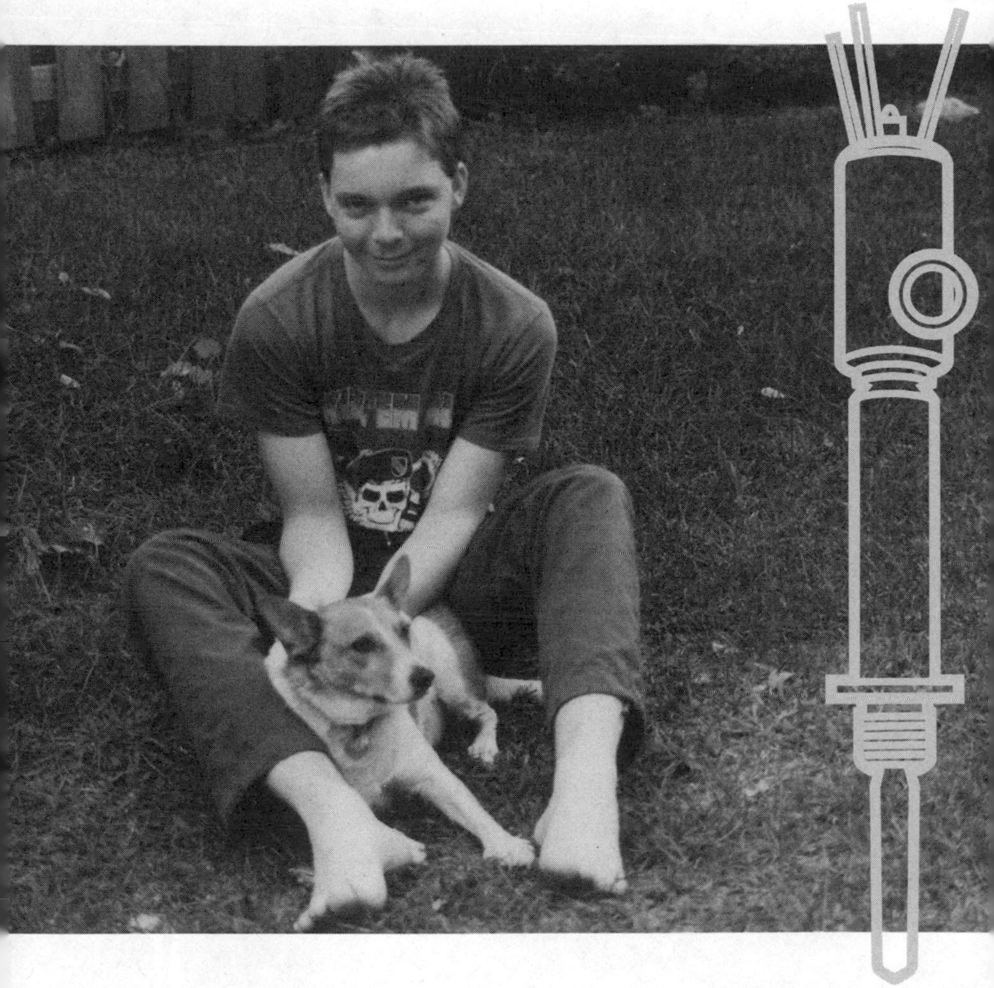

What I wanted was to be about 30,000 feet above the frozen ground. 30,005 if you included the trench I was busy digging. Mid-December in central Alberta and my world had shrunk to the specific size of a partially dug trench:
(8' x 5' x 3').

There is distant salvation in the clarity that a cold, cloudless sky can offer. The tip of the axe arced above the surface of the trench, a small and rhythmical signal of my presence. Against explicit orders one dug while the other napped. My fire team partner curled up in the snow while I was sneaking a look up, away from the task of around-the-clock digging.

Silent, slipping between the stars were two blinking lights, one red, one green. I imagined a passenger compartment full of dozing, cozy continental travellers. The seats reclined, maroon blankets covering sleeping bodies. I'm sitting amongst them, reclining with a blanket but not sleeping. Instead, sipping on a screwdriver on ice, I'm listening to my Walkman. Perhaps an early Pogues song like, *A Man You Don't Meet Everyday*. Perhaps I look out the window past the wing and down towards the dark, radiant blue of the snow-covered prairie.

What follows transpired before the fall, when we still gave a fuck; when guys sported maple leaf and **regimental** tattoos with no bitterness; when they didn't yet cut into their own arms with hunting knives.

So after Bill was [supposedly] jumped by a group from a rival **Battle School platoon** outside of The Wainwright Hotel, two things happened:

1. Word spread through the bar like, oh, crabs, and soon the whole place was fighting. Fighting for revenge, or retribution for revenge or, in the case of some, the realization that this was indeed a full blown, wild-west bar fight and that there was little left to do at such a time other than hurl a chair into the crowd, so they hurled a chair into the crowd.

2. Others, back at the base, layed low in a ditch and waited for other rival recruits to stumble back from drinking at the base bar. They attacked with broom sticks, fists and a sense of self-righteous vengeance and duty they hoped could some day be used to punish the enemies of our [once] passive nation.

Laundry night during Basic meant 194 pretty clean sheets gathered together and traded for 194 really cleans sheets. Meant the rarity of working with guys from the other squads vaguely glanced at during morning readings of *The Hero Book*. Meant enduring and indulging in all the lies.

On our course of 97 recruits, a lot of guys claimed to kick ass while folding sheets. These included:

Twenty-three black belts from a variety of disciplines
Eight martial arts instructors from a variety of disciplines
One ninja

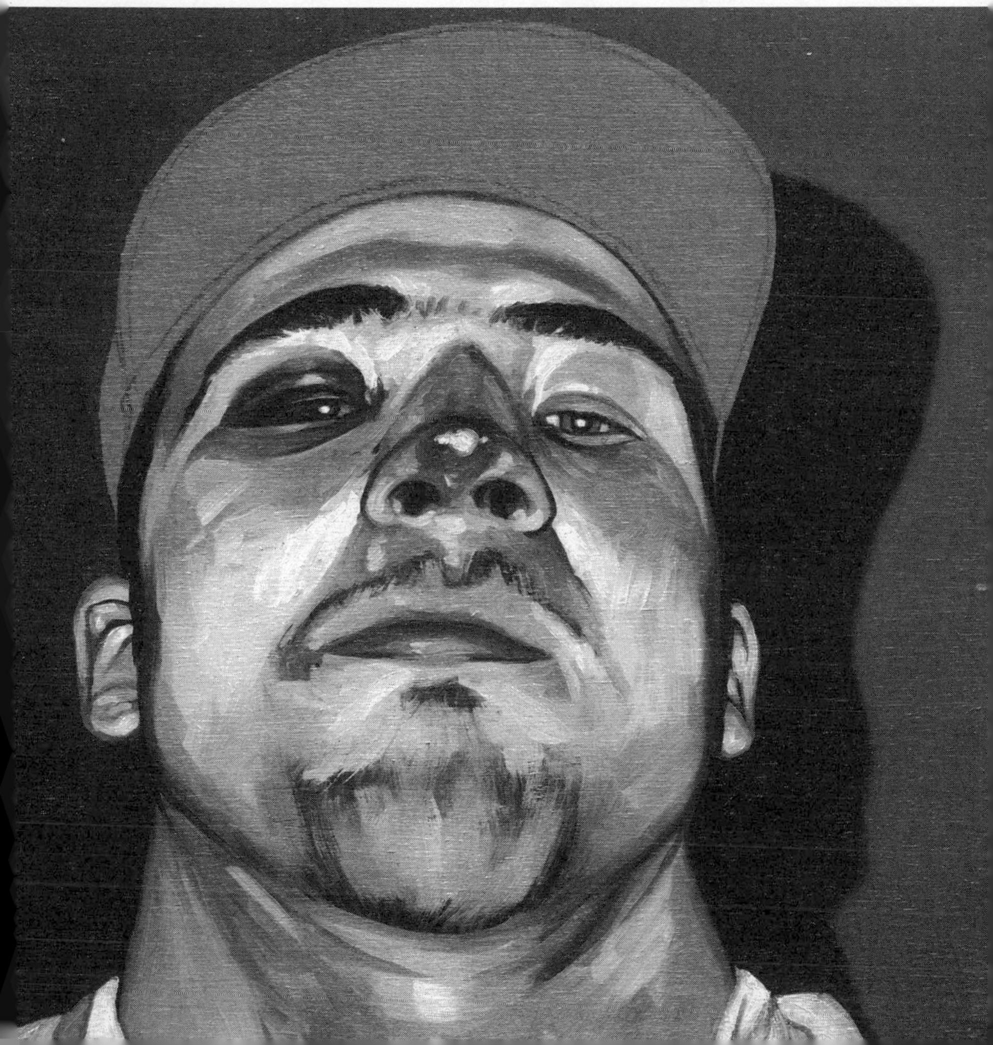

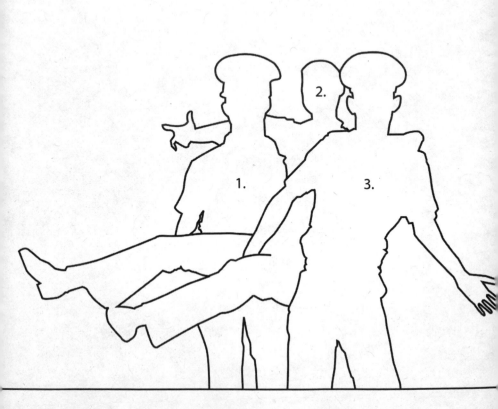

1. Is trying to be less of a flippant asshole and likes to accumulate letters after his name.

2. Currently, this fine fella teaches ESL in Surrey BC. He is happily married with two children though he no longer owns a cat named Tennis Shoe.

3. So far as is known, this trooper is a member of Canada's elite Commando/Anti-terrorist Unit, *JTF-2*.

Also of importance but not shown:

4. Moved well away from it all and lately has come home to roost as a prison guard [though I am sure there is a more pleasant sounding job title] to support his cute family.

5. Went on to get married, divorced and become an installer for an unnamed cable company. He is also an active member of the burgeoning *Lower Mainland Rapid Deployment Force* [also manned by #4].

6. Happily married with a small family, this *ex-Patricia* is a surveyor in southern Scotland.

7. This unrepentant smoker has worn many a hat over the intervening years and is presently occupied with an ESL gig in small town Japan. His family awaits his return to Alberta.

8. A former self-professed poacher of "The Queen's Deer," my old friend has dropped off the grid and has seemingly returned to poaching and sword-making on the South Shore of Nova Scotia.

Dicks

Part 1

Willy had an appropriate name.

I can only admit to having gotten drunk with him once. He was one of those ageing **Corporals** [or maybe **Master Corporal**, maybe] who stayed in because civvy life in New Brunswick wasn't worth going back to. He also really loved institutionalized drinking.

So anyway, a small group of us who weren't going on Brigade manoeuvres—due to the fact that we were getting the fuck out!!—went drinking at a downtown nightclub. Someone knew Willy and invited him along. He was good and pissed right out the gate and after not very long at all [another pun] he started his performance.

As different couples went out onto the packed dance floor, Willy would, with the flair and confidence of an old hand, casually walk around to where they had sat, unzip his pants and dip his cock in their drinks. Then he would saunter back to us and almost collapse with glee from his never-tiring prank.

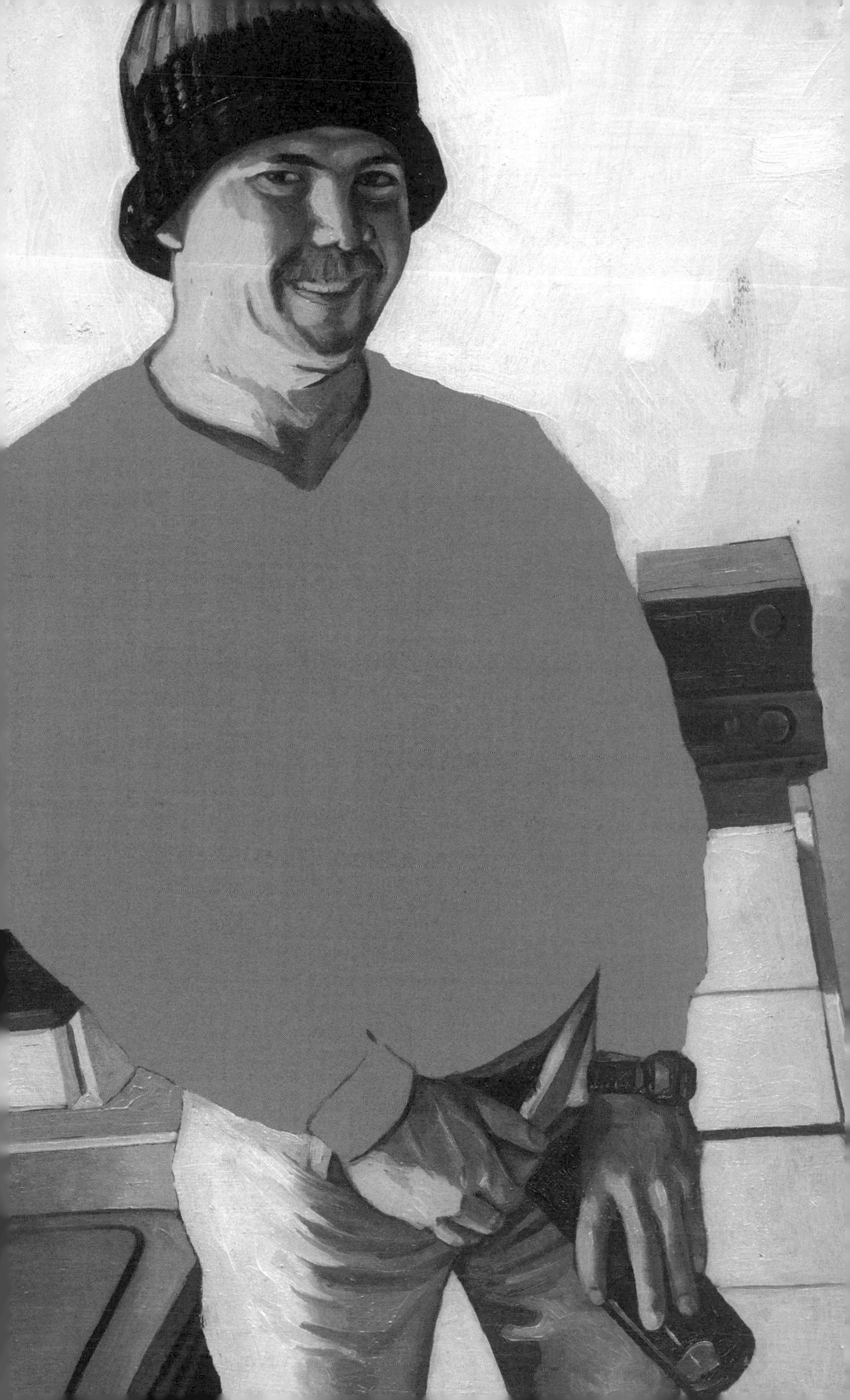

Part 2

Merlin's? Yes, Merlin's. Colin? Yes, Colin

Keeping track of the changing names hung on the numerous shitty nightclubs in military towns over a three-year period can wear a fella out.

Down on the waterfront, near the Parliament buildings, this particular establishment kept the same handle longer than most. Merlin's was a magical place indeed with its own fabled history. [By the way, this little yarn is hearsay, but my trust of Nicklehead has lasted to this day.]

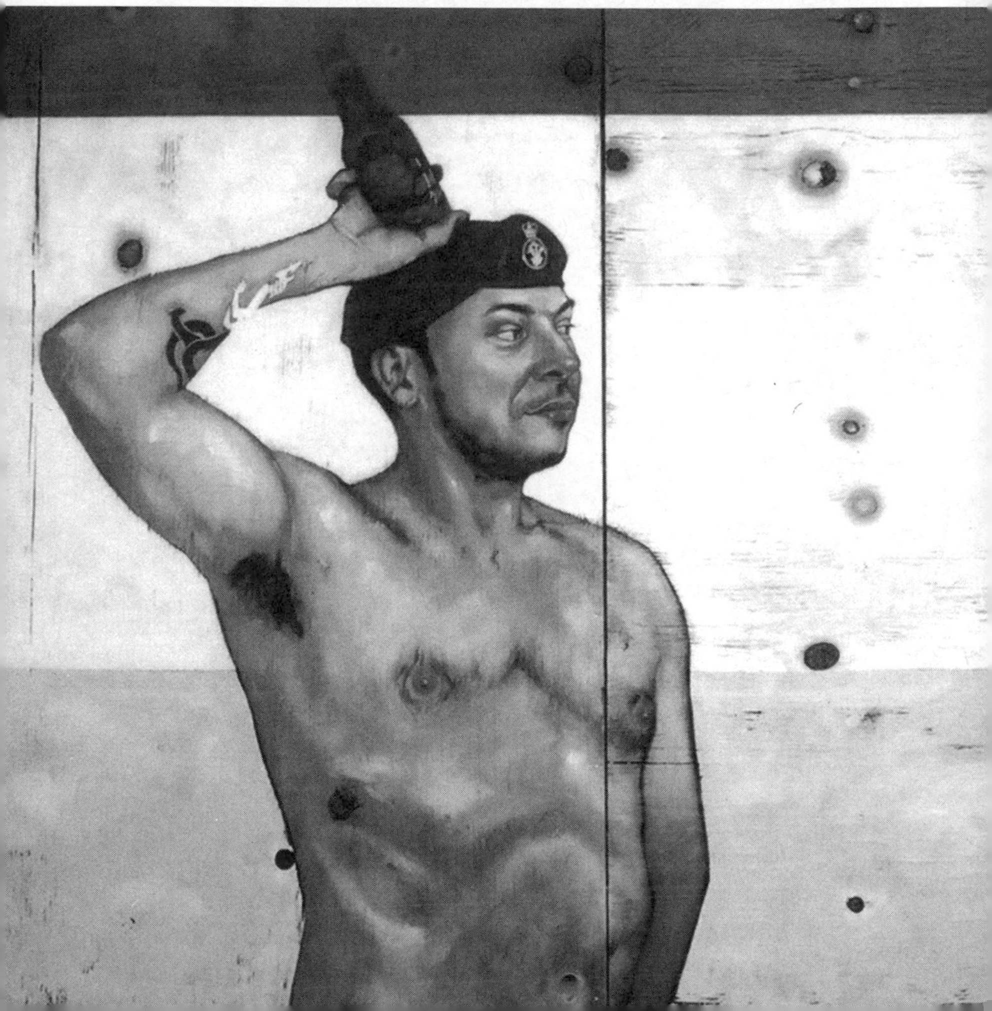

Colin could be an asshole of the highest denomination. He was kind of like getting a thousand-dollar bill; sure it's a thrill to behold but what the fuck use is it?

The story goes that some unlucky sailor [you know they are derided as lowest of the low, right?] was dancing with some girl as Colin danced next to them. The sailor bumped into him and, perhaps feeling his honour tainted by naval filth, Colin unzipped his pants and pissed on the sailor's leg right on the dance floor. Understandably the naval hero protested, but in Colin's eyes he should have taken the pee as his penance and called it even. Amongst the drunken throng Colin shit-kicked the sailor then walked away, leaving him crumpled and soiled.

Nicklehead tells me that Colin has been on the wagon now for a number of years, has a family and has become a decent sort. We are all assholes and are all, it seems, redeemable.

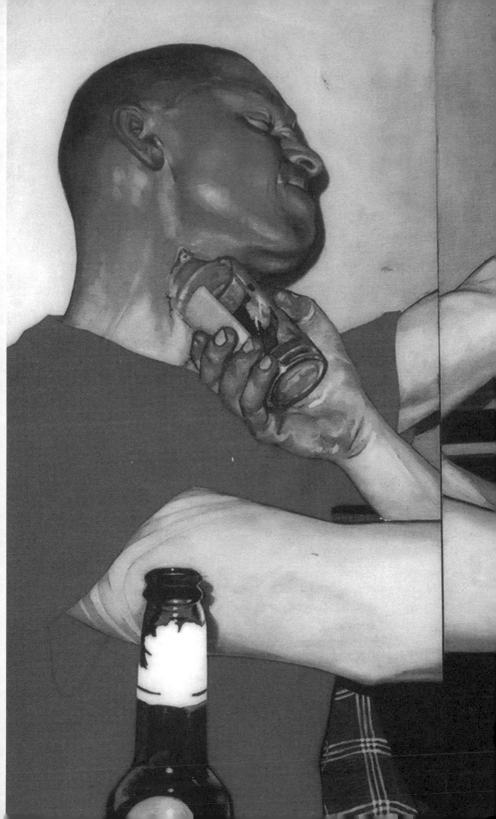

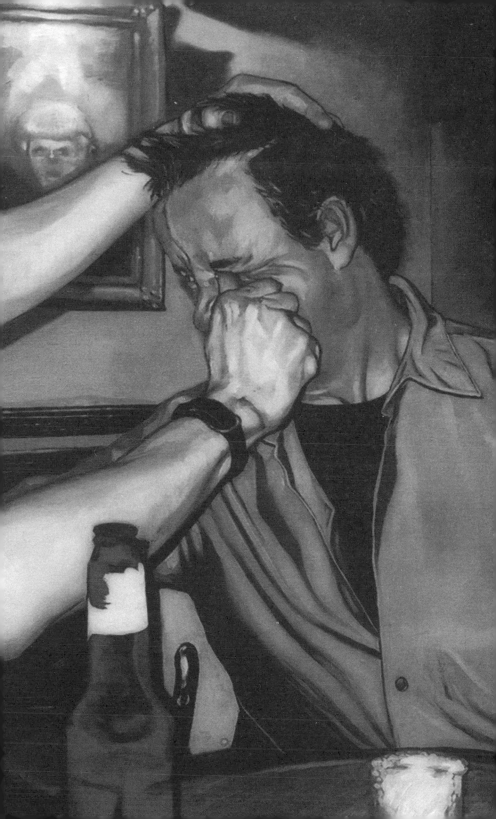

Perhaps this is all I need to show you.
Everything I've tried to drag back
across this chasm of time
can be distilled down to a hairless torso,
a farmer's tan and a GPMG.

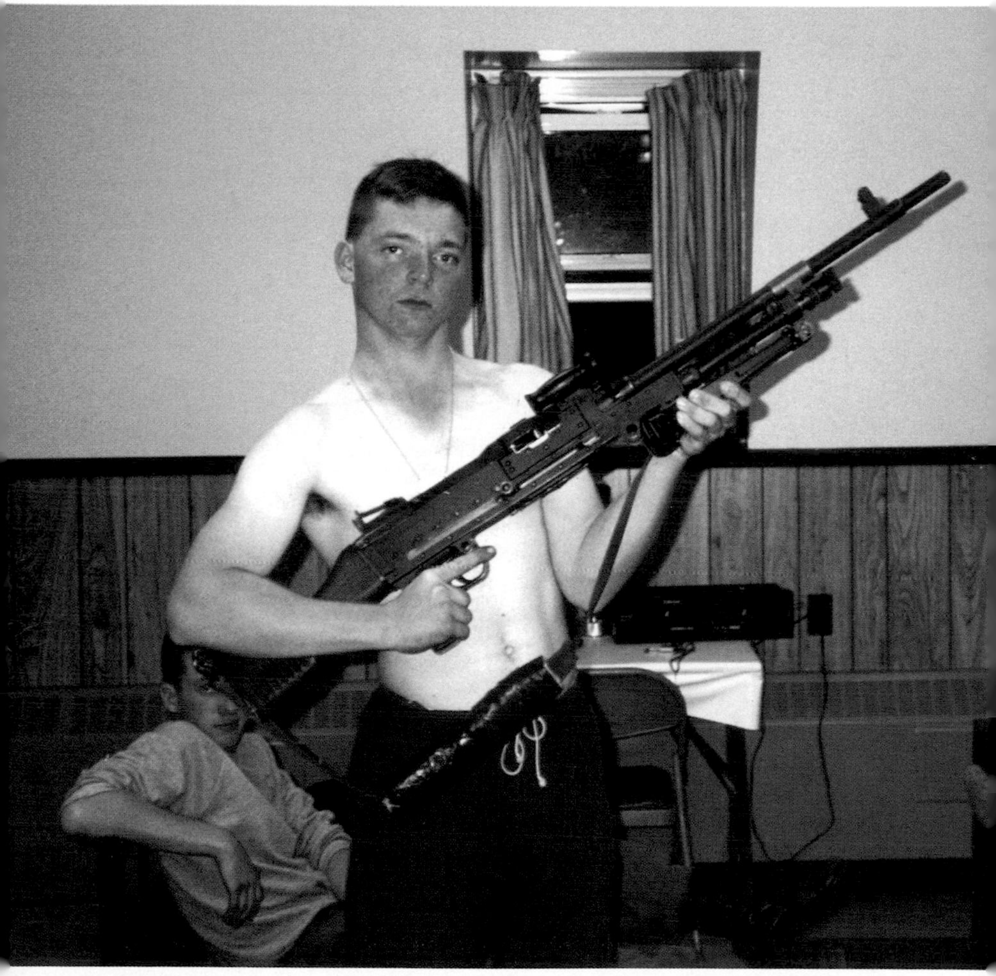

Sometimes referred to as ***Asshole with Pig***.

"Could it be that all war is basically sexual?...
A sort of sexual perversion?
Or a complex of sexual perversions?
That would make a funny thesis
and God help the race."

– James Jones, *The Thin Red Line*

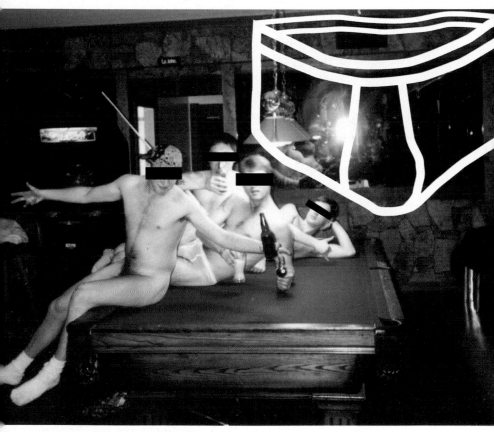

Members of the *22nd SAS Regiment* enjoy a beer
at the Hereford boat house.

A few years ago a small boy named Andy who had recently moved to the plains from Pennsylvania told me he knew an angel named Andy Le Beau. He spelled out the name for me and I asked him if the angel had visited him here. "Don't you know?" he said in the incredulous tone children adopt when adults seem stupefyingly ignorant. "Don't you know?" he said, his voice rising, "this is where angels drown."

— Kathleen Norris, *Dakota*

Dropping Away (flight)
a) 60 mm Mortar

Given the peculiarities of winter combat [staying warm in -20°C for example] you need to carry much more gear and weight, and there are times when it feels like this weight will crush your bones like a controlled implosion. There are, however, moments when you push through this pain, where transcendent bliss and clarity overtake you.

In addition to clothes, ammo, gas mask, shovel, frozen water, frozen food, sleeping bags, assault rifle, snowshoes, helmet, and a legion of sundry items, I was also carrying the platoon mortar. There's no easy way to carry the support weapons when in full battle regalia but one option for the mortar is to simply sit it across the top of your rucksack behind your neck, grab hold of the firing end of the tube then put your eyes forward and hump.

The austere, perhaps sublime beauty of the winter prairie has rewards beyond the aesthetic. If you are willing to carry 100 pounds or so on your back in complete silence through the long night, you achieve a realization that you are all alone with your pain, the pain refers only to itself and is, in fact, its own reward.

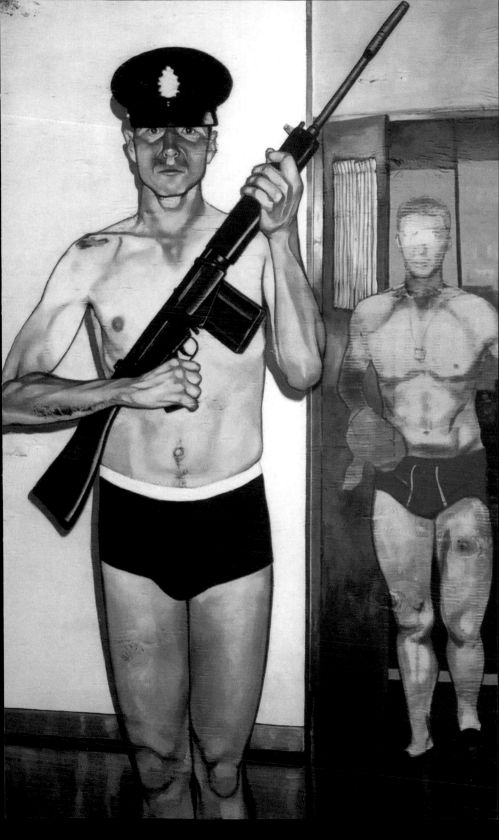

b) 99.44/100%

And now I am running across the steppe-sized expanse of night-time snowscape—a pursued blue-white speck upon the massive land. All the gear I carry is strapped down to eliminate noise [***tactical*** is the word] and, save for the crunch of snow under boot, I am nearly silent as I run.

There is, however, the small matter of the rattling, partially used bar of soap in its green plastic travel dish stuffed in the top of my rucksack. The noise of hard soap on plastic travels across the land unimpeded by natural buffers. Cleanliness, it seems, is not tactical and will be my undoing.

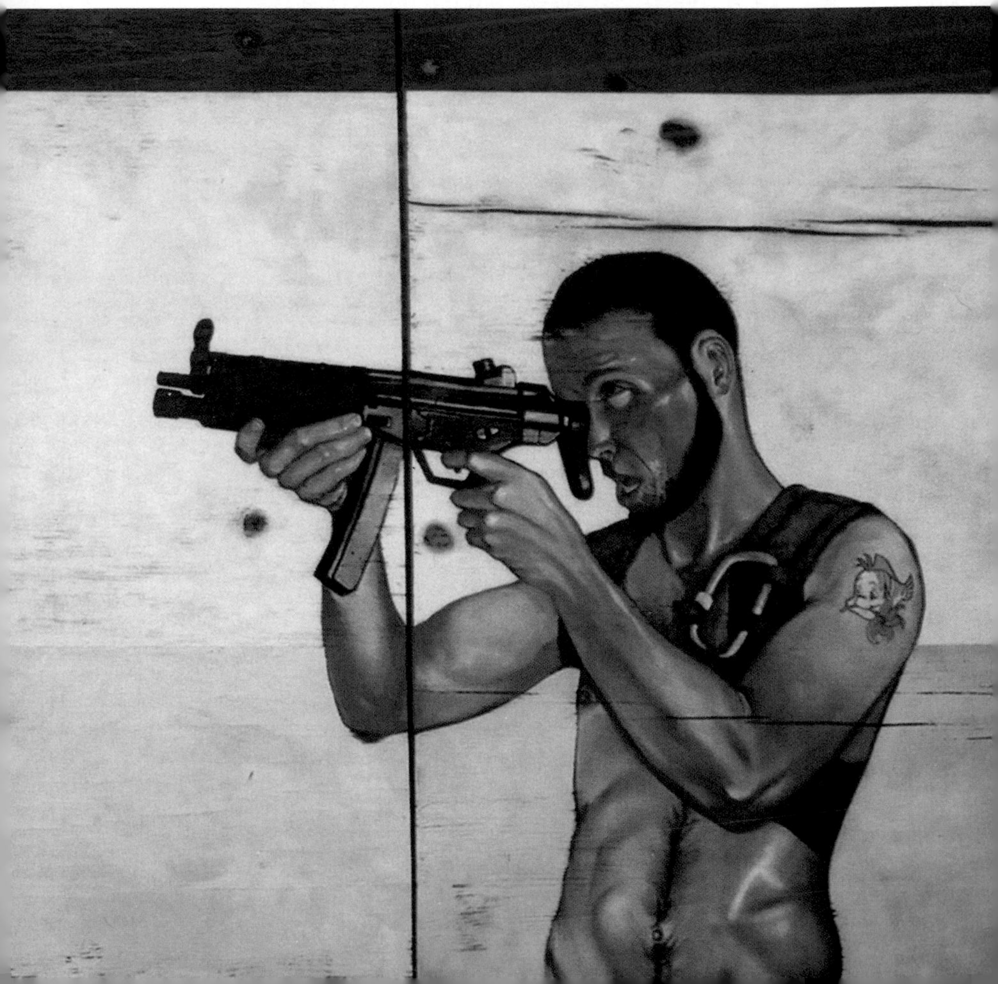

c) North West of Dakota

The "enemy" was still out there and I was thoroughly fucking lost. The moments of transcendence and physical determination were long behind me and now I really wished I hadn't split up with the small group I had begun this *escape and evasion* with, thereby forfeiting my access to a compass. Now with only a topographic map of this anonymous prairie, I felt close to useless. I walked on because there was nothing else to do.

Most large military bases [and Wainwright was certainly that] have expropriated land from farmers and ranchers over the decades, and it was a remnant of these acquisitions that materialized in front of me. Stepping over dilapidated wooden fencing I entered what must have been a corral decades before. When thoroughly lost in nature, any mark of man seems a welcome anchor [or sometimes a taunt] so I sat down amongst the crumbling timbers to take stock of my unsettling situation.

I removed the *winter-cammed* rucksack and used it as a pillow and layed on the snow. With my focus on the absence of topography, I hadn't looked upwards until now. Above me, the sky appeared split in half by an Aurora Borealis of such ferocity as I haven't since seen. If you consider the most elaborate Rorschach blot you might be able to conjure, invert it [white on black] and bring it to life as a dancing angel, wings spread wide, it might approximate what I saw. The entirety of the massive sky was transformed into a sublimity which was mine alone. At that moment I would have happily been taken up by that sky, a weighty mass of flesh, fabric and combat tools.

d) Final meal

I was on my knees, my hands were bound and a burlap sack covered my head. Inside the concrete-floored warehouse, there was the clomp of our interrogator's boots, and our own occasional moan, curse or mumble.

To call it torture would be egregious hyperbole—forceful interrogation would be more apropos. Specifics escape me, but the fluctuations of my will remain clear. Resilience comes and goes; depression, submission and abjection fill the gaps quite nicely. More than any of the previous challenges this is where you feel most alone, most helpless. You know well enough that others are bound and blind all around you, but contact is not at all condoned. Instead you focus on, then attempt to ignore, then focus on the pain shooting up from your knees as you kneel on cold concrete for hours at a time. As your will fades then returns, anger can be harnessed to keep you going through the silence of the floor and occasional sessions with the interrogators.

Also though, you know goddamned well that this is all just a training exercise and you feel totally fucking betrayed by the **NCO**s [they are now your interrogators] who have previously treated you like shit, called you down, built you up, made you strong but never betrayed you. Fuck you!

Then it is over. The hood is removed, your hands are freed and you look around to see who remains and who broke. You are fed cold, green oatmeal and it remains the best fucking thing you ever ate.

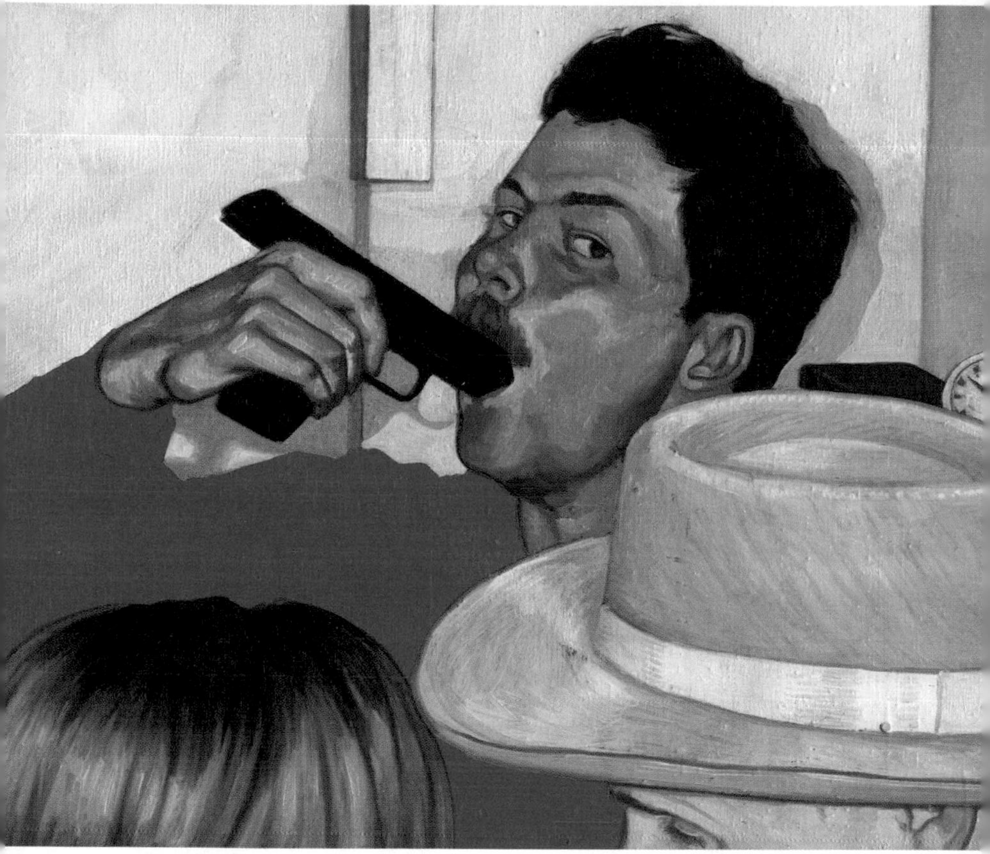

Also: One guy [not pictured here] failed the ***Final Ex*** and was subsequently sent back to another platoon to do it all again because he took his section's last packet of sugar, thereby depriving his sergeant of sweetened coffee. He was a fuck-up and a butt shark though, and many of us were pleased that in this case there seemed some justice in the universe.

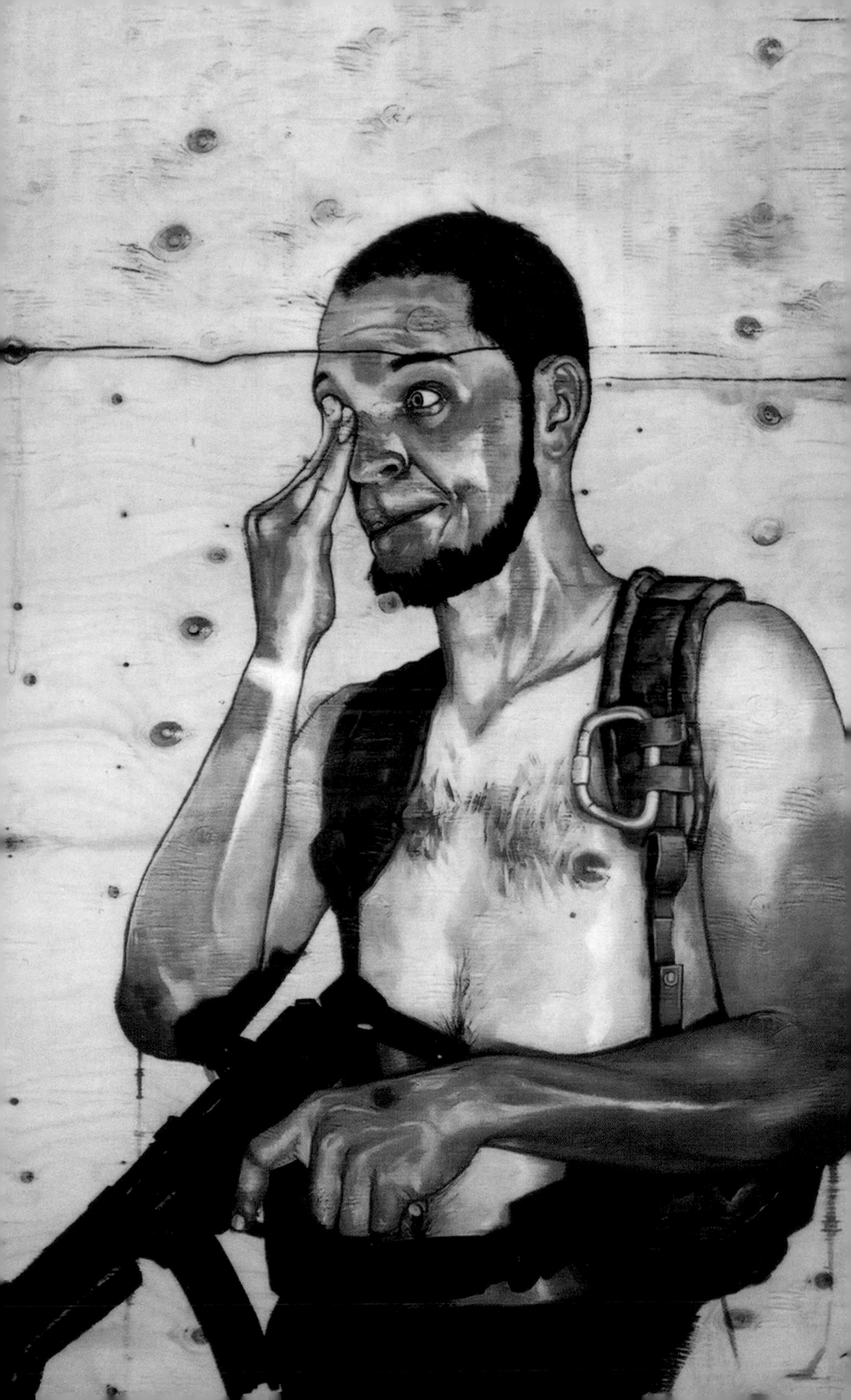

I quite clearly recall crouching in the hall outside the platoon room. I was leaning against the pale green, mildewy wall as a two-four was being passed around. The beer [probably Kokanee or Canadian] seemed a token attempt at dulling the resentment we were feeling from being 'bugged out' to do a fighting patrol on the weekend.

I refused the beer as a display of the depths of my despair. Beer was the fucking blood of Christ as far as the infantry was concerned, and to turn it down was an overtly suspicious act.

Squatting there in an abject rage, covered in a weekend's worth of Sooke's muck and swamp, I said to myself: "Don't ever forget this feeling; how much you hate the fucking army. Sit here and remember this fucking feeling."

Also: Twelve years on and there is no way to conjure up the ferocity of those feelings. What remains is an anthropological endeavour. Digging through the rubble of so many degrading and empowering acts, so much drunken debauchery and base misanthropy—all that remains is a catalogue. While catalogues are useful for shopping lists and Christmas wishing, they are abjectly incapable of rekindling any semblance of the rage.

Now's your moment
Floating in the blue lagoon
Boy, you better do it soon
No time would be better

"What a great fucking movie," I often thought to myself back in the winter of 1990. So did the guys I was stationed with.

We knew the songs and dialogue by heart and knocked back beer, vodka or sometimes rubbing alcohol and would pause the scene where Ariel ascends, in her now human form, to the world above. After a few hours of drinking we would head down the hall to the communal showers to get cleaned up for the prairie girls who would later be in the bars, as drunk and desperate as we were.

First though, we would wash our hair and lather our bodies. Taking our drinks with us, the soundtrack tape would be turned up loud enough to echo around the shower walls and through the steam. I would sing along with Dacon and Prevachal and swill Black Label and we would sometimes pee on each other.

Darling it's better
Down where it's wetter
Take it from me

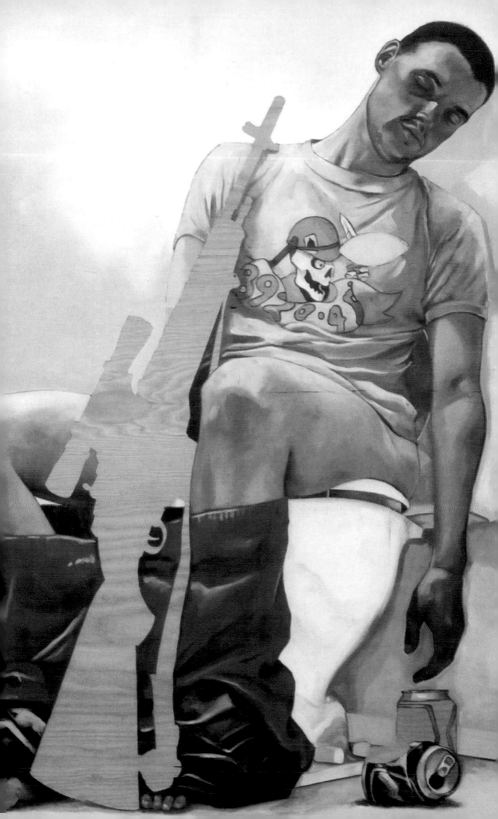

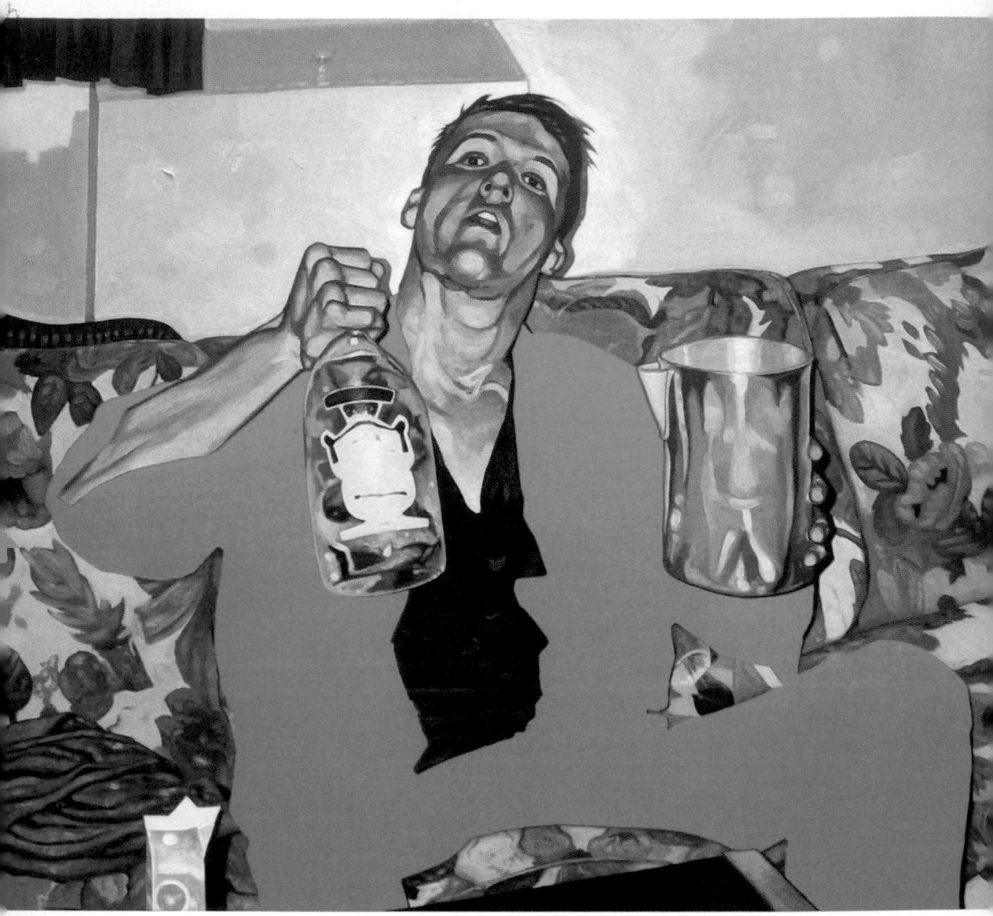

More a Sabbath fan than the Blizzard of Oz or solo Ozzy years, I do, however reserve a soft spot for *No More Tears.*

Mike had the room across the hall from Biff and myself. He had also come into a set of bar speakers which were large enough for me to sit on and dangle my feet. On the weekends Mike would inevitably come back very late from the Esquimalt bars—often The Halfway House—and start repeatedly pumping out *No More Tears.*

The music made it far too loud for all but the drunkest to sleep, so I'd go across the hall [Biff would be sleeping] and sit around with Mike and a couple of other stragglers and we would knock back whatever he had left over.

Usually the selection was fairly bleak and I would often end up with Tequila and hot chocolate powder—a better option than the rubbing alcohol or even cologne I sometimes drank.

Perhaps this is a good opportunity to mention that Mike had the God-given gift of large foreskin. He sometimes entertained small groups by filling it up with as many quarters as possible. Supposedly he once managed eight dollars worth.

Also: While we're in Mike's room I should recount an incident involving a guy in my platoon named Neil. Well drunk, he was ranting on about the evils of alcohol; about how it was wasting our youth and corrupting us and didn't we see what was happening to us. After a short while, he grabbed someone's 40 of CC and threw it out the third floor window. It cleared the barbed wire fence and plunged down to the residential street outside the base. It didn't break though. Neil ran out the room, appearing on the street about five minutes later. There he picked up the booze and smashed it good and proper.

There are stories of some armies in South America giving their soldiers German shepherd puppies to raise and nurture. After a year they are forced to kill their dog to prove their mettle as killers.

Canada's version was to give us each a grouse. Those feathery critters were thankfully in our lives for little more than an hour—less time than they would spend in our bellies. While most of our platoon was allowed to chop their heads off with an axe, my section participated in a tribute.

Our section commander, *Master Corporal* Tuttle, was an ageing skid and a huge fan of Black Sabbath, so as a tribute to Ozzy we were ordered to bite the heads off the live birds. As my teenage teeth sank into the grouse's neck I was mostly surprised at how warm and soft it was. [Imagine biting into a heated, feathery Twinkie.] Perhaps the hollow bones helped.

Though much has faded, I can close my eyes right now [right now] and feel the warmth, the fuzziness and the ease with which I performed my first kill for the infantry.

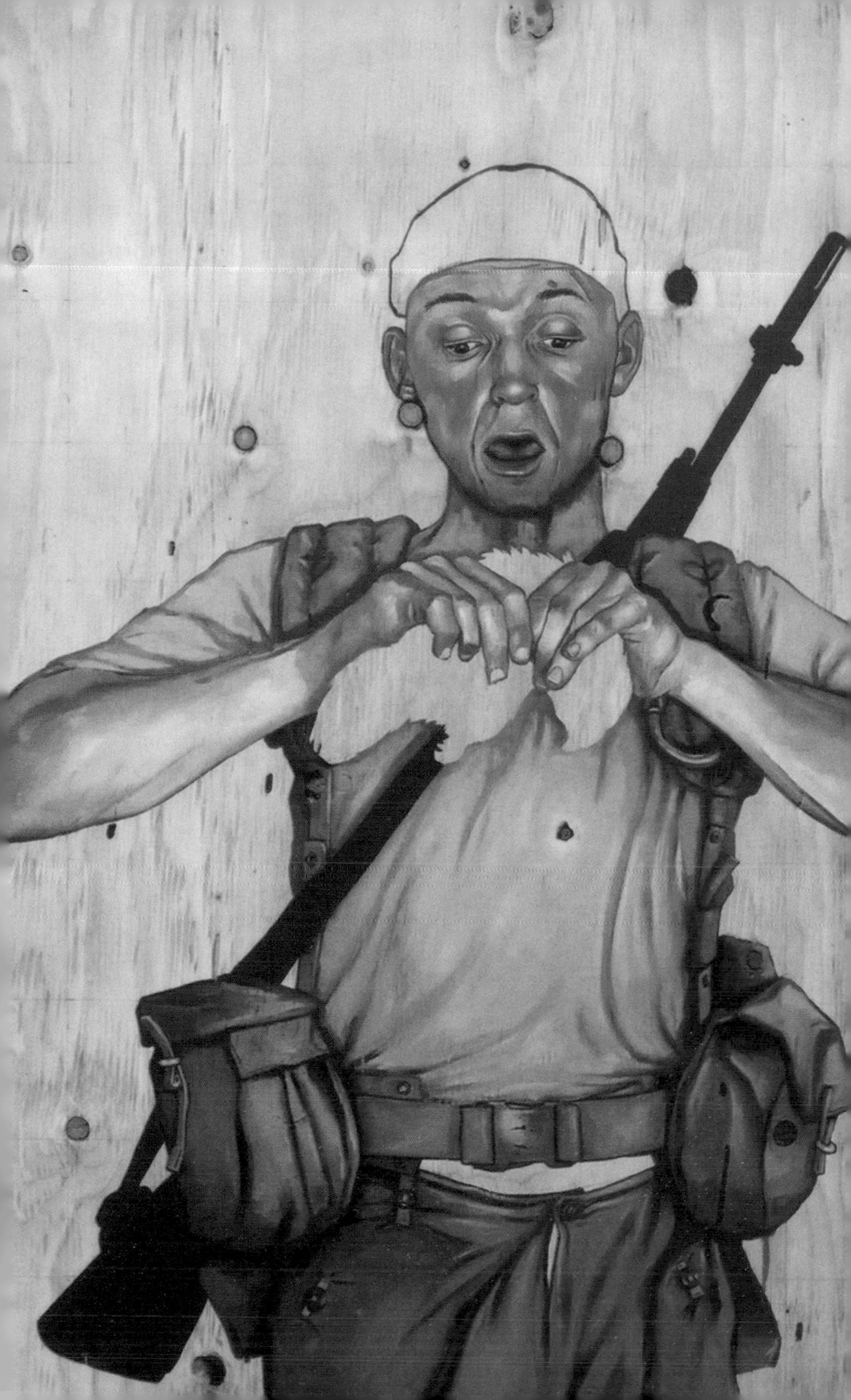

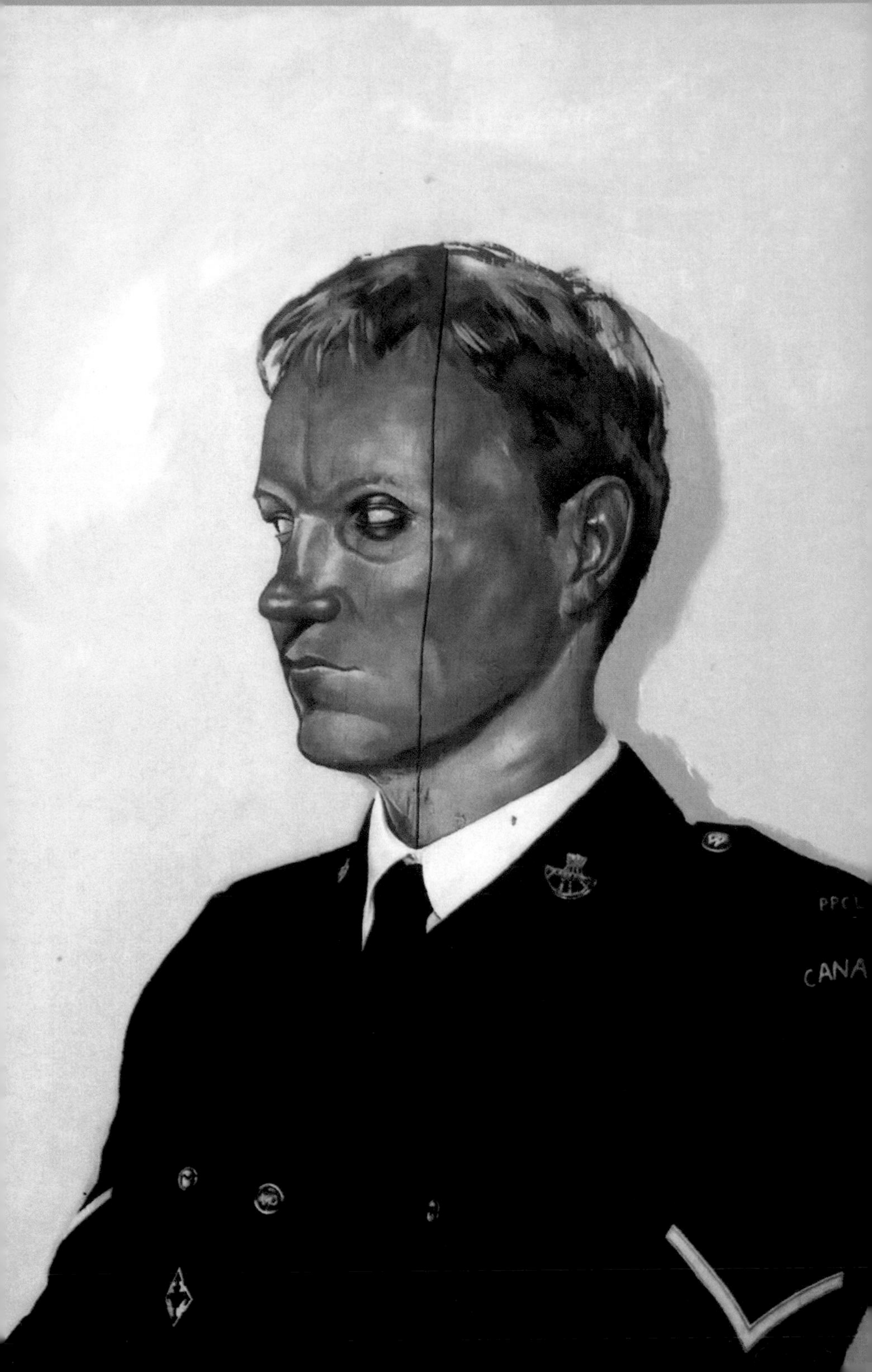
PPCL
CANA

"Dear Mom:
It snowed today. Bullshit, that is." *

* Quote courtesy Nicklehead's letter home.

I think it might have been a fighting patrol or something longer and wetter up in Sooke, the night the war began.

This was the same patrol where one of the **NCO**s hid a 20-pound slab of slate in the platoon commander's rucksack as a practical joke. While quietly tittering over the Lieutenant* humping the slab for days we sat in the soggy, dark confluence of temperate rain forest and the Pacific Ocean listening with a concoction of anticipation and dismay as the radio operator whispered the opening moves of *Operation Desert Storm.*

A few months back we had given up any hope of participating in the war. Weekends of revolver shopping in downtown gun stores were brought to a pre-emptive halt by the Prime Minister's pronouncement of "No ground troops." That was the final lump of dirt on our mass grave.**

From then on we grumbled our way through knee-deep swamp, knowing that this training amounted to shit and, really, we should be drinking more heavily and more often.

* As we descend from a British military system, the word should please be pronounced *Leftenant*.

** Forgive the hyperbole—Sometimes it's all that works. There should, in fact, be a disclaimer at the start of all military memoirs absolving the author of all criticism in this regard.

Callout: **"What makes the grass grow?"**

Return: **"Blood makes the grass grow!"**

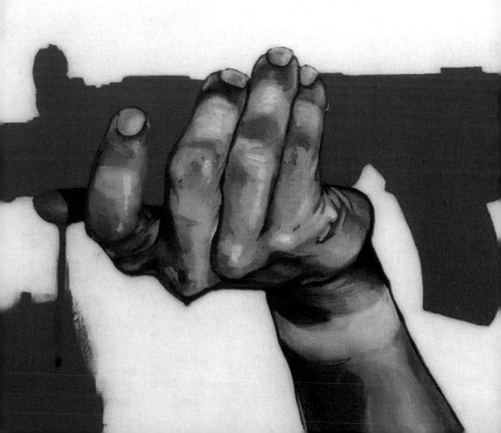

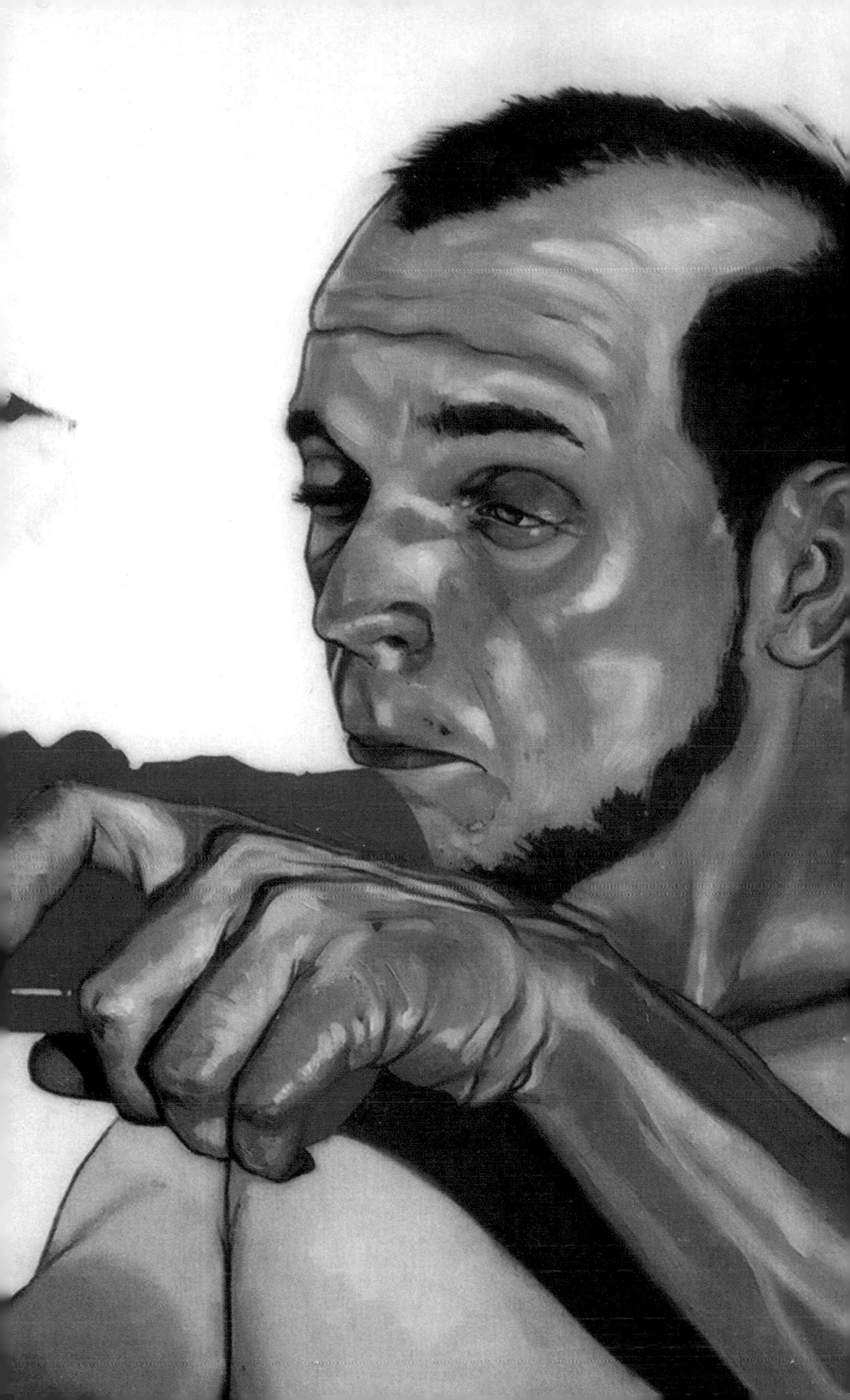

There was the time when Jay tried to bite the tip off some guy's nose in a bar fight.

Or how about when our **Battalion** was up at Mount Washington for a **Winter Ex**. The exercise had finished and our platoon was allowed to go into Comox for the night. We took a transport truck and drove to a local shithole bar.

While we got pissed, Jay and some local guy spent their time staring each other down across the dirty tables and blue air. As usual, this posturing came to its inevitable if undiagnosable head and they went outside. With his posse of bar chicks and sycophants in tow the local guy prepared to fight by taking his jacket off.

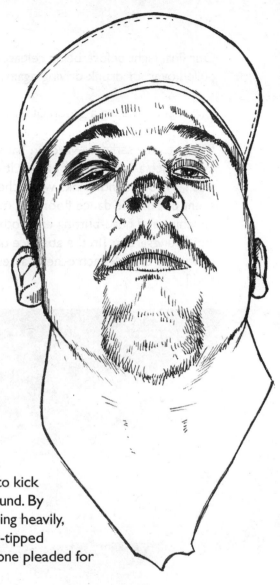

Jay grabbed the guy's jacket
collar and pulled it over
his head, blinding him. After
suckering him in what was
probably the jaw, Jay began to kick
the guy as he lay on the ground. By
now unconscious and bleeding heavily,
Jay layed into him with steel-tipped
Cowboy boots while someone pleaded for
him to stop.

Pent up rage or frustration was not a motivation, and I
won't offer that excuse—Jay was just a tough fucker from
Scarborough who loved his friends and liked to kick the shit
out of anyone foolish enough to try taking him on.

Our final night before being released ended with my getting pulled over for drunk driving again.

Earlier that evening a group of us short-timers, Dave, Brian, Bernie, Steve and myself, went across the Johnson Street Bridge to the same downtown bar where penis dipping had taken place a few months earlier. It was mid-week, so the place was fairly quiet and drinks were cheap. Much of our time was spent out on the dance floor in a mosh-pit of our own making, punching and head-butting each other to Jane's Addiction and Soundgarden. [In the absence of an enemy to fight, we continued to kick each other's asses until the looming, bitter end.]

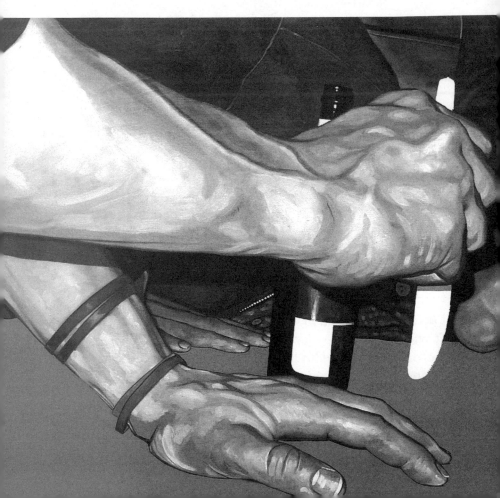

At closing we piled out of the bar. A taxi was dropping two couples off as we walked out the door, and as one of the guys in the quartet stepped out of the cab, Dave suckered him, knocking him out cold. As he was laying in front of me on the concrete sidewalk. I started kicking him in the face while his girlfriend screamed.

My friends let me believe I had kicked his eye out, but I only broke his nose, they told me years later.

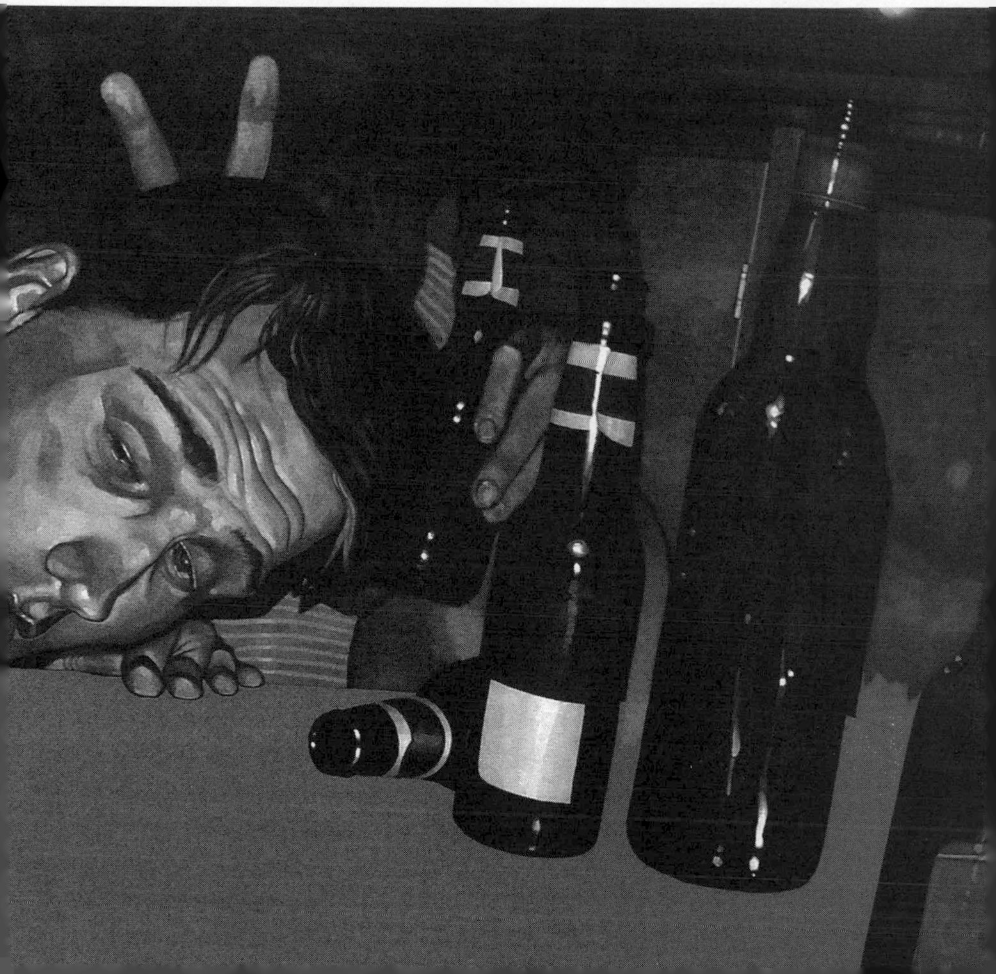

Callout: **"He served his country well."**

Return: **"And so shall we!"**

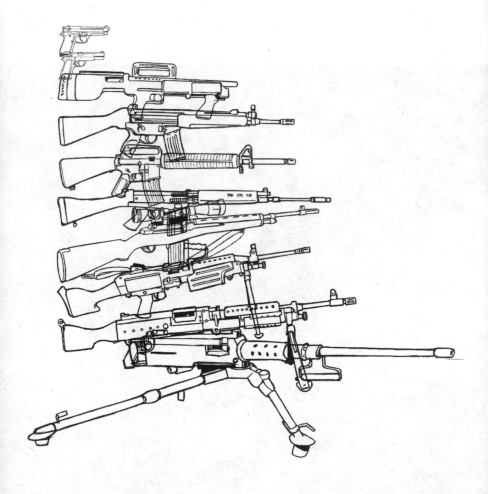

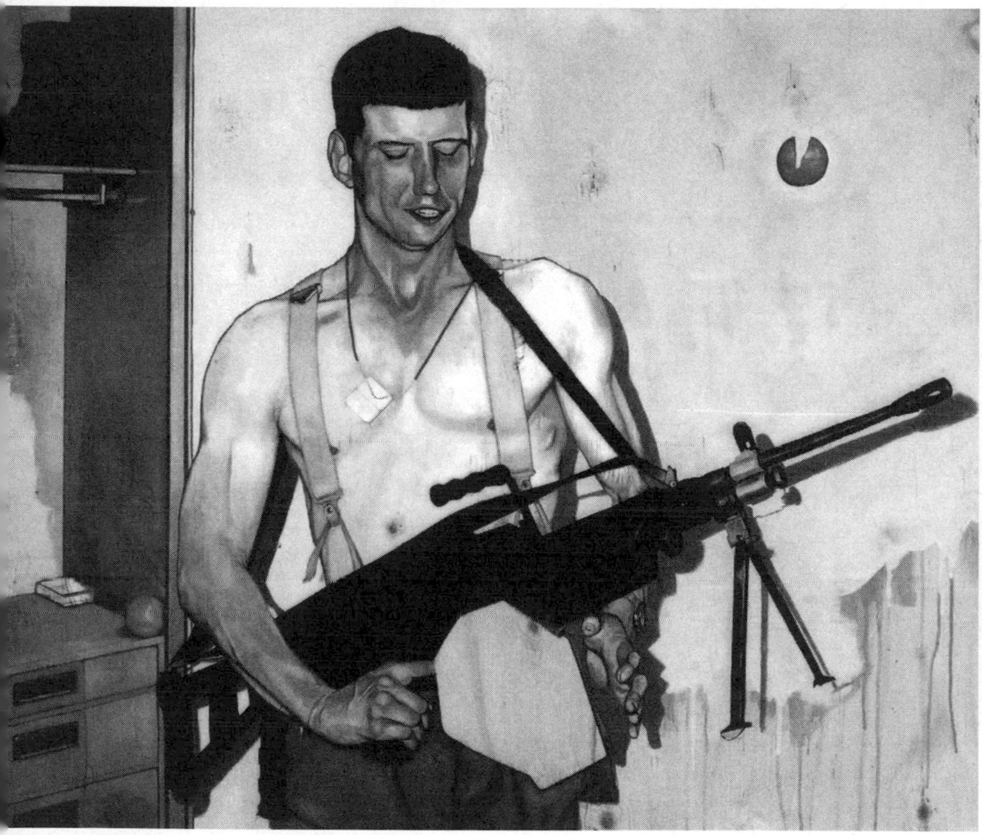

Most of the firearms I have ever used
[not to any really accurate scale].

08.05.92

After getting out in May 1992, a large group of us left the insulation of The Island and created a support group amidst the heat, gated retirement communities and two-fours that defined Kelowna.

Dave came up to visit us shortly afterwards. He shot up Highways 5 and 97-Charlie on a brand new 750 cc Ninja courtesy of The Insurance Corporation of British Columbia. From a whiplash claim, Dave had used his $26,000 settlement on the Ninja and then, upon arrival in Kelowna, pizza, booze and hookers* This was all well and good and great—Dave sending us to the liquor store with his open wallet—until the toilet backed up.

All those hookers and all those used condoms flushed down the loo gave us a basement an inch deep in our own backed up waste, but thankfully there was more booze and stale pizza and, anyway, only a couple of us lived in the basement.

A few months later, back in Victoria, the cash blown, Dave crashed and totalled the Ninja.

* Dave didn't share the girls.

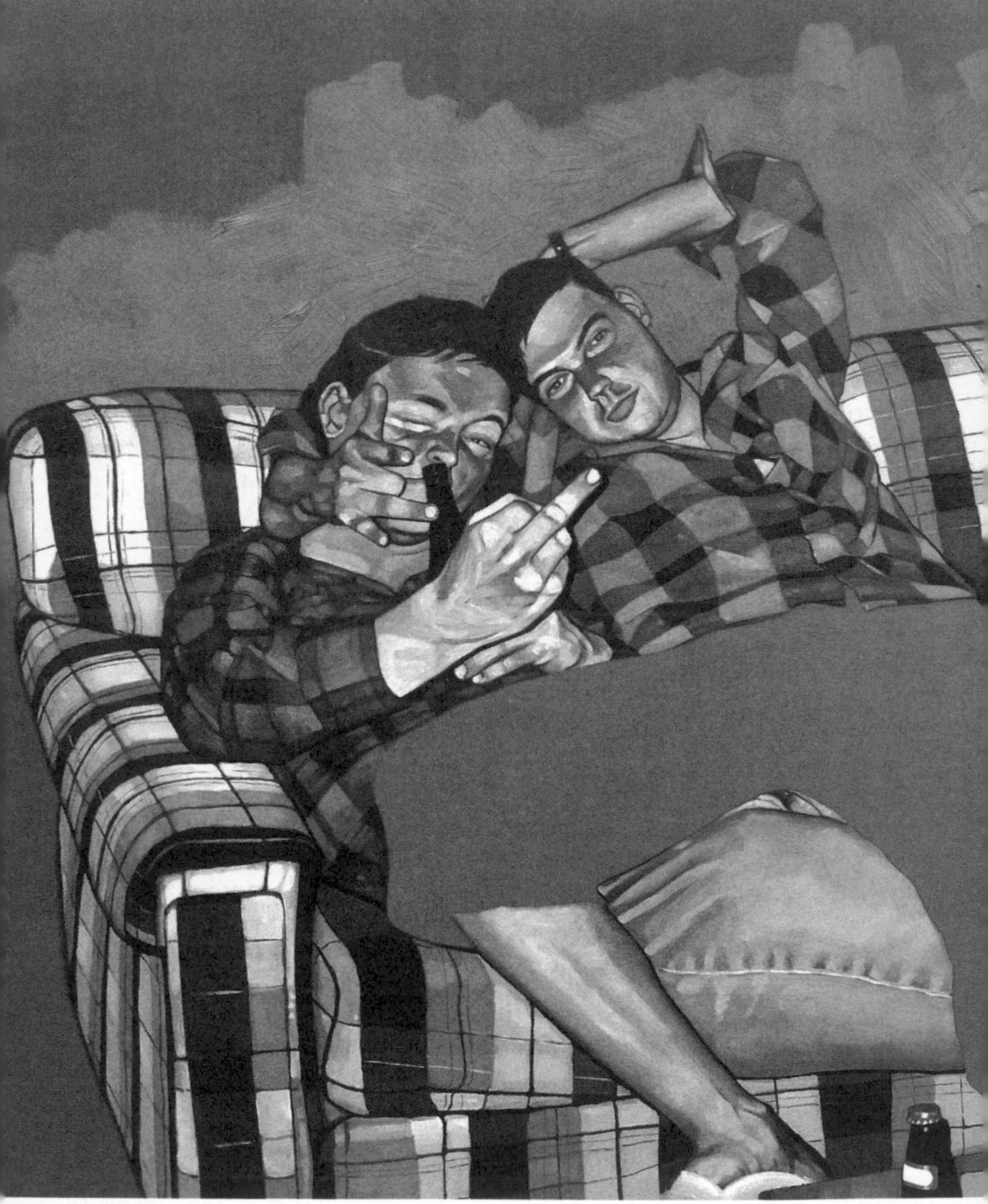

1. **sorry**

2. **fuckin' A**

3. **uhh...**

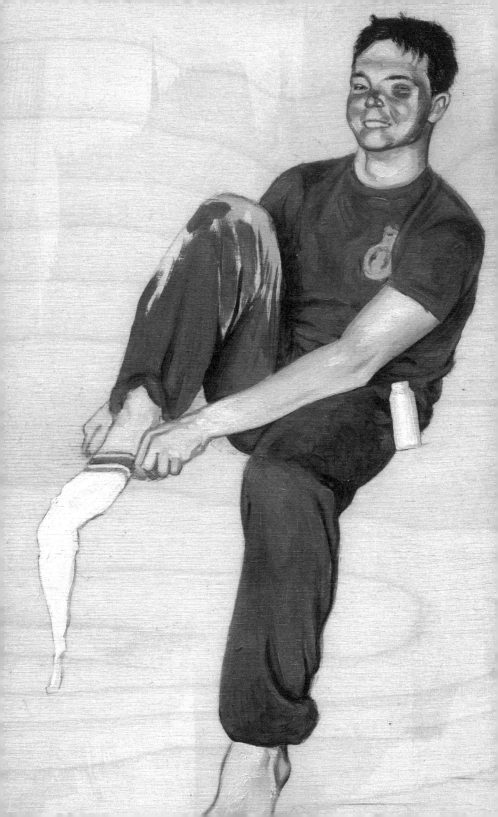

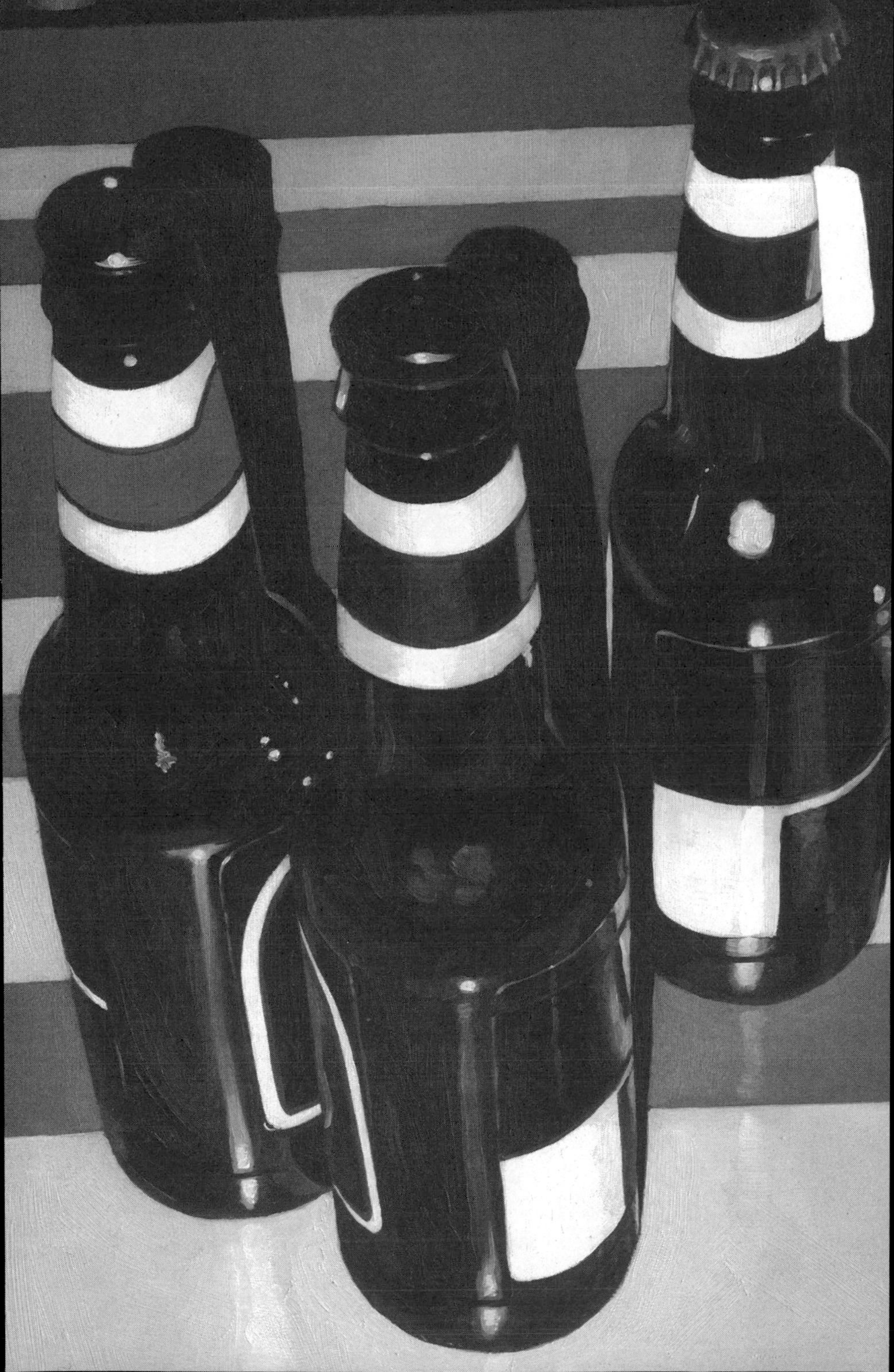

It's nice if you can
come through trauma
having learned
something useful.

Z — zulu
Y — yankee
X — x-ray
W — whisky
V — victor
U — uniform
T — tango
S — sierra
R — romeo
Q — québec
P — papa
O — oscar
N — november
M — mike
L — lima
K — kilo
J — juliet
I — india
H — hotel
G — golf
F — foxtrot
E — echo
D — delta
C — charlie
B — bravo
A — alpha

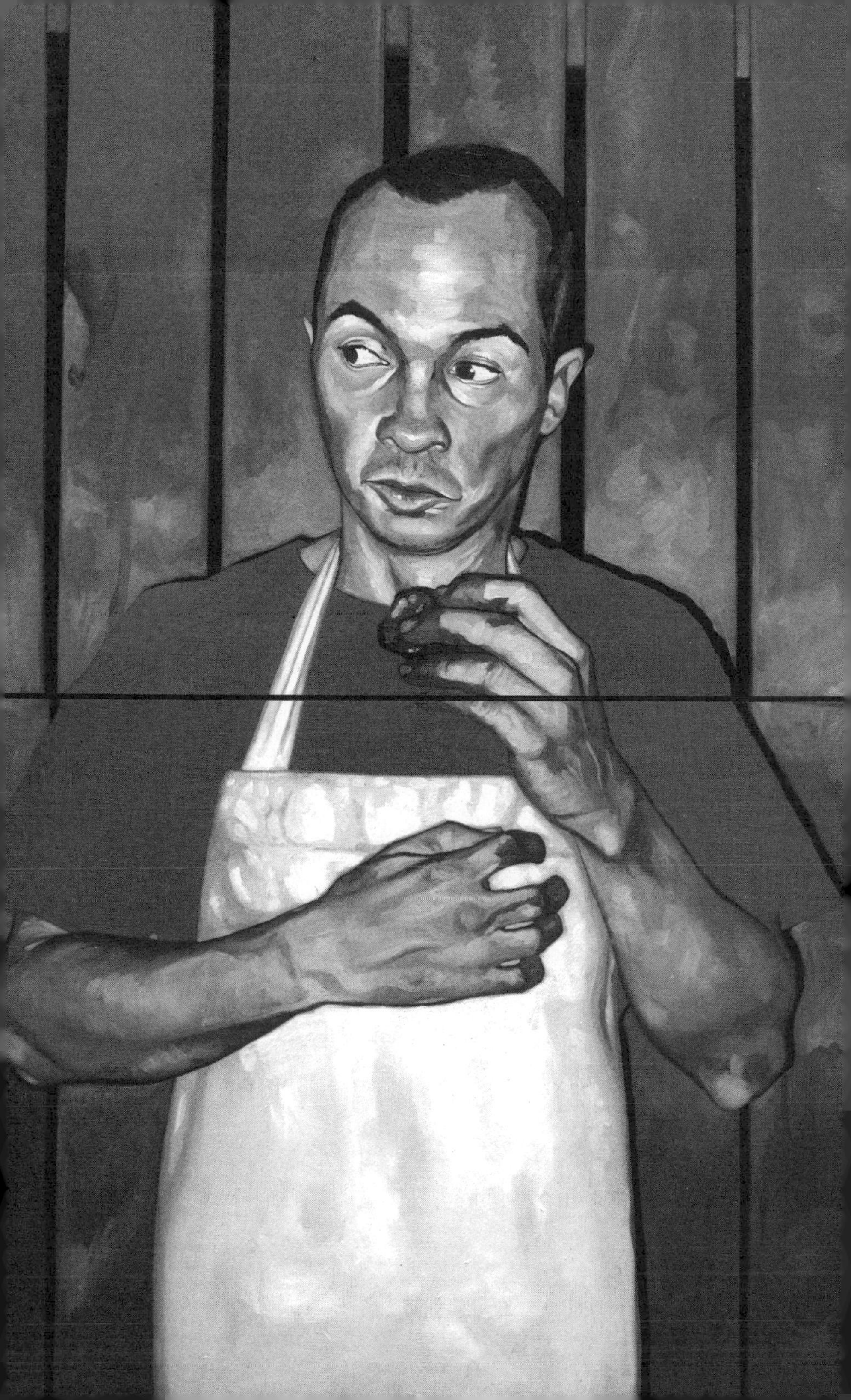

A Note and Acknowledgements

Note: I've changed some names in the preceding pages.

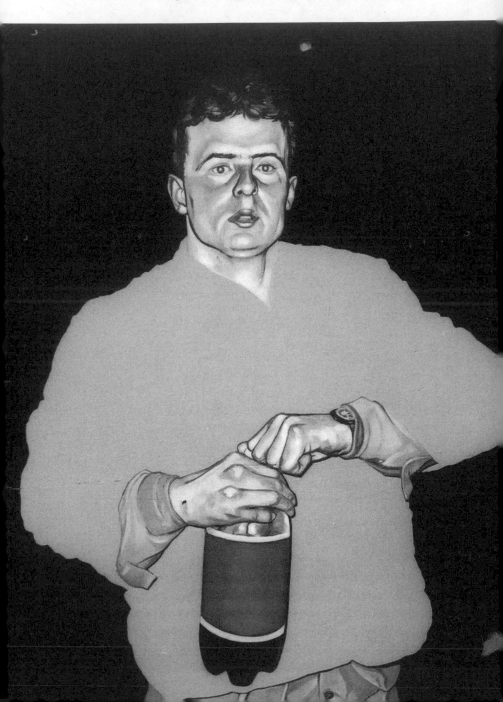

Thanks to: The members of 3 PPCLI and especially those who arrived via 8908 "Pursuit to Mons."

John Lent and Michael Turner for offering up the power of simple prose forms.

The Ontario Arts Council for their financial assistance in the production of some of the paintings in this book.

My York University MFA Committee: Michel Daigneault, Janet Jones and especially David DeWitt for helping me step back through the looking glass to understand how [I believe] it all went wrong.

Stephen Andrews for offering the word "homosocial."

Lastly and perhaps most importantly, David Widgington for his commitment, enthusiasm and investment in publishing this book which stands in my stead.

[And Jim Munroe, for reasons too vague to list.]

Bibliography

They helped me. You might like them:

—Crawford, John. *The Last True Story I'll Ever Tell.*
New York: Riverhead Books, 2005
—Dyer, Gwynne. *War: the new edition.*
Toronto: Random House Canada, 1984, 2005
—Grossman, Dave. *On Killing.* New York: Back Bay Books, 1995
—Hickey, Dave. *Air Guitar.* Los Angeles: Art Issues Press, 1997
—Jones, James. *The Thin Red Line.* New York: Delta, 1962
—Kaplan, Danny. *Brothers and Others in Arms.*
Binghamton: Southern Tier Editions, 2003
—Marin, Louis. *Utopics: Spatial Play.*
Atlantic Highlands: Humanities Press, 1984
—Mumford, Steve. *Baghdad Journal.*
Montréal: Drawn & Quarterly, 2005
—Norris, Kathleen. *Dakota.* New York: Mariner Books, 2001
—Richter, Gerhard. *The Daily practice of Painting.*
Cambridge: The MIT Press, 1995
—Saint Exupéry, Antoine de. *Wind Sand and Stars.*
New York: Reynal & Hitchcock, 1939
—Sassoon, Siegfried. *Memoirs of an Infantry Officer.*
London: Faber and Faber, 1930
—Sontag, Susan. *Regarding the Pain of Others.*
New York: Picador, 2003
—Swofford, Anthony. *Jarhead.* New York: Scribner, 2003
—Turner, Michael. *Hard Core Logo.*
Vancouver: Arsenal Pulp Press, 1993